MERRY CHRISTMAS

IMAGES
of England

SOUTHALL

Charles Price Abbott (1894-1973). Abbott (seen here in ceremonial robes) was very active in local affairs. As chairman of the Independent Rate Payers' Association, he was Deputy Charter Mayor in 1936. He resided in Dormers Wells Lane with his wife from 1924. He owned the Iron Bridge Service Station and was an authority on beekeeping. He was awarded an MBE in 1962. (See also p. 40.)

IMAGES
of England

SOUTHALL

Compiled by
Jonathan Oates

TEMPUS

Tempus Publishing Limited
The Mill, Brimscombe Port,
Stroud, Gloucestershire, GL5 2QG

ISBN 0 7524 2268 5

Typesetting and origination by
Tempus Publishing Limited
Printed in Great Britain by
Midway Colour Print, Wiltshire

This book is dedicated to my parents

The coat of arms of the Borough of Southall was granted in 1936. Trees are a common part of many Middlesex coats of arms. The trees here are thorn trees. Note that the wording is in English: most Middlesex coats of arms are in Latin.

Contents

Acknowledgements

I would like to thank the following persons, namely Mr W.H. Bignell, Mr J. Gauss, Miss M. Gooding, Dr P. Hounsell, Mr P. Fitzmaurice and Mr G. Twyman, for proof reading this work and for enabling me to avoid many innocent blunders. Any remaining errors are my responsibility alone.

I would also like to acknowledge the kind permission of Ealing Library Service for allowing the bulk of the photographs which appear here to be reproduced. Other photographs have been borrowed from Mr S.S. Bilga, Mr R. Samra, Dame Cleo Laine and North Road Primary School, Southall. I would like to thank them all for their kind permission to reproduce them here.

Principal Sources

Ordnance Survey maps, 1865-1935
Middlesex, King's and Kelly's directories, 1860-1937
Henry St John's diaries, 1930s-1940s
Census Returns, 1851-1891
The Southall News, 1885-1888
West Middlesex Gazette (and subsequent titles), 1935-1965
Southall Council Minutes, 1936-1965
Southall Guides, 1930-1964
Southall Local History Transactions, 1959-1968
Kirwan, P., *Southall: A Brief History*
Victoria County History for Middlesex, Vol. IV
Meads, R.J., *Southall, 1830-1982*, and *Growing up in Southall from 1904*
Twyman, G., *The Martin Brothers*

All these are available at Ealing Central Library.

Introduction

This is not a history of Southall. Rather, it is a collection of images showing aspects of Southall's history from the mid-nineteenth century to around 1965, when Southall became part of the newly created London Borough of Ealing. I cannot but help quote Dr George McDonald, who wrote the foreword to Samuel Short's quaint booklet, *Southall and its environs*, in 1910. McDonald wrote, 'Like all children I looked over the pictures first, and I recognised many buildings of bygone days, becoming fewer every year from the ravages of time and the jerry builder, and in future it will be a pleasure to all who possess this book to know that so many of these interesting relics have not been removed without some momento of them being preserved'. Such comments are equally applicable ninety-one years later.

Southall is nine miles to the west of the centre of London. It is a scattered parish, with Norwood Green one mile and a half to the south of Southall railway station. It reaches as far north as Ruislip Road, with Greenford to the north and as far east as the River Brent, bordering on Hanwell. Hayes lies to the west of Southall, the boundary being the Yeading Brook and Heston lies to the south.

By way of introduction, a brief outline history of Southall will be attempted. It should be noted from the outset that Norwood is the name of the ancient parish; though Southall is the name by which this part of the current London Borough is known. The earliest known reference to Norwood is found in the will of an Anglo Saxon priest called Werhard in AD 830. Little is known of Medieval Southall. Since it was part of the manor of Hayes, owned by the Archbishop of Canterbury, it was not mentioned individually in the Domesday survey of 1086. Indeed, up until 1859, Southall was not a parish in its own right, but a precinct of the parish of Hayes. Southall/Norwood had but 106 years of relative independence before once again becoming consumed by a larger unit of local government.

Norwood was spelt *Northuuda* in Werhard's will of 830. By the Middle Ages it was *Norwode* and by 1724 it was Norwood as we know it today. Southall itself was first referred to in documents in 1198 as *Suhaull* and underwent various name changes in following centuries, such as *Southolt* and *Southolde*. The 'South' part of the name is to differentiate it from Northolt. It is unclear where the 'North' part of Norwood comes from, unless it means to the north of some long-vanished wood.

Like most parishes in Middlesex, Norwood was a small farming community, made up of several scattered hamlets; Norwood, Northcote and Southall. In the early seventeenth century, peas and beans were grown and sheep grazed. At the end of the eighteenth century, arable farming was dominant. The only local industry was brick-making, which began in 1697, and lasted until the early twentieth century. In 1801 Southall's population was only 697.

However, in the nineteenth and twentieth centuries, change was rapid, as it was for the surrounding parishes. Much of this was encouraged by the innovations in transport. The building of the Grand Junction and the Paddington canals at the end of the eighteenth century and the coming of the Great Western Railway in 1839 encouraged industrial development. Even so, it was not until after the First World War that many of Southall's roads and streets were built.

Two important families in Southall's history, members of whom will be referred to in the captions, were the Abbotts and the Villiers, who went by the title of Jersey. The Abbotts lived in Southall since the eighteenth century and were involved in local politics, business and other activities. Charles Nash Abbott founded Southall's first newspaper in 1885. The Jerseys were a noble family who owned much of the land in Southall. They lived at Osterley Park, just outside Southall.

Many of Southall's industries were household names; including Quaker Oats, AEC and Taylor Woodrow. In 1961, AEC was the largest single employer in Southall, employing 5,000 workers. These three firms all set up in the interwar years. Over half of Southall's work force was employed in local industries in the 1950s.

As we have seen, until 1859, Southall and Norwood were administered by Hayes. In 1859, Norwood Vestry oversaw parish events and, amongst other matters, created the drainage system. In 1894 the Southall-Norwood Urban District Council was formed, which lasted until 1936, until replaced by Southall Borough Council, which dropped Norwood from its name. The Borough Council came to an end in 1965.

After the Second World War, Southall's character changed out of all recognition. So much so that a recent (1999) council guide to Southall declared, 'For a more exotic experience, stroll the streets of Southall and imagine yourself in Delhi'. Immigration, largely from the Indian sub-Continent, began in the early 1950s. By the time of Southall's incorporation into the London Borough of Ealing, in 1965, the immigrant population in Southall numbered about 9,000.

Although there have been other books which have shown images of old Southall, most of those presented here have not been previously published. There are also extracts from the diary of a former resident of Southall, and he will now be introduced. His name is Henry Algernon St John, 1911-1979. St John was a civil servant and a bachelor, who kept a diary from 1922-1968, which is now held in Ealing Library. In these diaries there are some interesting passages which throw a light on social life at the time. St John resided in Saxon Road in the 1930s. References to extracts from the local press have been taken from *The West Middlesex Gazette*, which covered Southall from 1923 to 1941, and its successor, *The Middlesex County Times*.

There are several histories of Southall, though none are currently in print. However, they can be read in Ealing Local History Centre in Ealing Central Library or at Southall Library. The most scholarly account is that found in *The Victoria County History* of Middlesex, Volume IV. It gives a detailed account of social and economic history. Easier to read, yet still very good, is Kirwan's *Southall: A Brief History*. Less good, but still useful, are the books by R.J. Meads, though they are somewhat anecdotal.

Jonathan Oates
August 2001

One
Roads and Streets

Southall, from an etching by George Barrett (died 1784), c. 1770. This is the earliest known picture of Southall and is possibly of the Oxford (later Uxbridge) Road. This was an important route for stagecoaches and other transport travelling from London to Oxford. The many public houses *en route* marked important stopping points.

King Street, looking northwards from the junction with Norwood Road, early 1900s. Named after the nearby pub The King of Prussia which was renamed The Victory during the First World War. The original name appeared in 1814 when the Prussians had been our allies in the struggle against Napoleon.

Poplar Cottages, looking northwest, c. 1905. In 1891 gardeners and labourers resided there. Note the shed in the foreground is partially demolished.

Alexandra Avenue, shortly after it was built, early 1900s. The road is probably named after Queen Alexandra, 1844-1925, who was Queen to Edward VII. As recently as 1896, a brick field covered the site of this street, and all that land north of the Broadway.

Muddy Lane, c. 1910. Part of this became Allenby Road in 1930, named after General Edmund Allenby (1867-1936) of Near East fame. Its rural appearance is a reminder that many of the 'roads' in Southall would have looked like this in the nineteenth century. As the local press observed in May 1930, 'But why change the name at all? To keep the old name would be a pleasant reminder of the days ... when the villagers named their names with graphic simplicity. The fact that there will be no longer enough mud in the road to justify the name is no objection.'

South Road, looking north to the Broadway, c. 1910. Hamilton Road can be seen branching to the east. In 1865 there were very few houses on South Road. By 1896, most of the east side of the road had been built up, but it was not until 1914 that houses began to be built on the western side of the road.

Norwood Green Road, looking east, 1924. This is a very old road, dating back to the eighteenth century at least. Between 1865 and 1935, unlike the rest of Southall, this part was almost totally unchanged; with houses on the north side of the road and with the Green opposite.

South Avenue Gardens under construction, *c.* 1926. South Avenue Gardens was one of many housing estates laid out by the council between the wars. Up to 1914, a brickworks had stood on this site.

South Avenue Gardens on completion in 1927. Only the road and the pavements need further work.

Ranelagh Road, 1932. Work began on Ranelagh Road in 1927. It may have been named after Viscount Ranelagh, an eighteenth-century philanthropist, but the local connection is unknown. In the nineteenth century a brickfield covered much of the land which is now south of the Broadway, including the site of this road. The brickfield was connected to the Grand Junction Canal by a dock and canal branch.

North Road, Mount Pleasant Estate, under construction, 1930s. At least until 1865, North Road was bordered by trees. On 28 December 1930, Henry St John noted, 'Walked to the Iron Bridge. Noticed more new houses in course of erection at Mount Pleasant, by the contractor Wimpey. All north-east Southall is being covered with new houses, into Greenford.'

Cornwall Avenue, from Allenby Road, after road resurfacing in the 1930s. The road was built in around 1931. Before the 1920s, all this part of Southall was fields.

Townsend Road, c. 1933. Built in the 1900s the road is named after the demolished Townend House (see p. 28). However, it is not on the site of that house, which was to the west of the top of South Road and to the south of the Broadway. Townsend Road is a long street running south from the Broadway to Beaconsfield Road, to the west of the site of Townsend House.

Lancaster Road, unsurfaced, *c.* 1930. This was one of a number of roads in Northcote ward named after periods in English history, from Saxon to Tudor. The House of Lancaster provided monarchs from 1399-1461 (Henrys IV-VI). All these roads were built north of the Broadway in the first three decades of the twentieth century. The road was built in the 1900s, the houses on the western side of the road being built first.

Trinity Road, 1930s. This road was built in the 1900s. It is not thought to have been named after Holy Trinity church as some have imagined. Note the gasholder in the background.

Wimborne Crescent, Norwood Green, *c.* 1930s. The man on the bicycle has obligingly halted his journey for the benefit of the photograph. The notice board for Warren and Woods is a reminder of a local building firm that had premises in Norwood Green, as did Holly Lodge Laundry, whose sign can also be seen on the right.

Mount Pleasant Cottages, the Common, shortly before they were demolished to make way for flats in the 1950s. These houses were built in the 1860s and originally housed bricklayers, gardeners, servants and labourers and their families.

Longford Court, Uxbridge Road, c. 1953. These low-rise flats were clearly the pride of Southall Council. Pictures of them appeared in several of the official Southall guide books in the 1950s. They were a mixture of one and two bedroom flats, thirty-six flats in total, costing £68,282 and completed in July 1953. The architect was the Borough Engineer, Mr S.F. Thorne.

The Plough Inn, Norwood village and the approach to the Green, 1958. The contrast between this scene and others in this chapter is clear. The Plough Inn dates back to at least 1845 and predates The Plough in North Road by at least fifteen years.

Two

Houses

The Beehive, Mount Pleasant, c. 1880. The house is probably mid-nineteenth century in origin. John Clark, beer seller, resided here in 1881. He was sixty at the time and was born in Buckinghamshire. His wife, Caroline, was fifty-nine.

Southall Manor House, perhaps the most important building in Southall, in 1887. It is certainly the oldest. Built in about 1587 for Richard Awsiter, it remained in his family until 1821 when it was purchased by William Welch. Later owned by the Thomases and the Scarisbricks. It ceased to be in private hands after 1912. The first institutional owner was the council, followed, in 1970, by the Southall Chamber of Commerce.

Southall Manor House, central hall, *c.* 1900. The fireplace is attributed to Grinling Gibbons. The arms above the fireplace are those of the Awsiter family, the house's original owners.

Mr William Frederick Thomas, sewing machine manufacturer, born 1830, and owner of the Manor House, is seen here, probably, in the 1890s. Thomas occupied the house from 1879 until 1895. He was a great local benefactor. In the winter of 1885·1886, when there was extreme poverty due to unemployment among the brickfield workers, he provided penny dinners for up to one hundred poor children per day. He was also president of the Southall Cottage Gardens Association and served as Norwood's first County Councillor in 1889.

Mrs Fanny Thomas and her dog, in the 1890s. Mrs Thomas was born in Paddington in 1843.

Manor House Bailiff's Cottage, *c.* 1890. This dated back to the seventeenth century and was located at the back of the Tithe Barn. It was used as a presbytery for the Catholic church. After it fell into disrepair, it was demolished and the site used to build a new school.

Scarisbrick family in the gardens of Manor House, *c.* 1900. The Scarisbricks occupied the house from 1898-1912, before selling it to the council for £6,100. They allowed the tithe barn to be used by a priest to say Mass. The young girl in the photograph, Emmanuel, was born in 1888 and became a nun. She and her brother, Father Gerald, were invited by the new owners of the Manor House, the Chamber of Commerce, to visit their old home in 1970.

Hill House, Mount Pleasant, c. 1890. Built in around 1858 for Mr William Welch Deloitte, (1818-1898) chartered accountant, it was claimed that this house commanded, 'one of the prettiest views in Middlesex'. As well as founding one of the largest British accountancy firms and becoming immensely wealthy, he also gave money to Holy Trinity church and founded six almshouses (see p. 29).

The Baxter Family at Home Farm, The Green, c. 1890. In 1891 Henry Phelps Baxter (centre), aged sixty-four, was the head of the household. He was a farmer and butcher and was born in Southall. Others seen here include his wife, Julia, his mother-in-law (seated), Mrs Simmons, born in 1806, and his unmarried daughters, Henrietta and Malvira. The cleric is Henry Cole, from Ireland, Baxter's son-in-law, married to Alice. The smaller children are their offspring; Bessie, Charles and Edith.

Vine Cottage, Park View Road, seen here in the 1890s, was probably built in the 1850s. It was bought by Charles Thomas Abbott, 1859-1905 (see also p. 60), manufacturer of bee hives and uncle of Charles Price Abbott, in 1885. A youth club was later built on its site.

A Vine Cottage bedroom, in the 1890s. Interior photographs from this time are rare.

Northcote House and Park, South Road, in the 1890s. It was built in around 1666 for William Leybourne, mathematician and scientist. In 1896 it was occupied by George Gibson, a builder, who was chairman of the vouncil, 1898-1899. The house was burnt down, but the park was developed as a public amenity in the 1920s.

Old Cottages at the junction of North Road and Meadow Road, c. 1900. The cottages probably date from the early nineteenth century.

Featherstone Hall, Southall Green, 1901. It was built in the 1870s on the site of a farm house for Alfred Welch (son of William Welch). This new building was dubbed Welch's Folly, on account of the high walls around the house, interspaced with windows, built at a cost £20,000. By 1891 it was a lunatic asylum for ten wealthy female inmates, presided over by Hephzibah E.E. Dilson. The Hall was demolished in 1935 to make way for The Dominion.

Brickmakers' Cottages, North Hyde, in the early 1900s. There were many brickfields around Southall in the nineteenth and early twentieth centuries. Their exploitation was stimulated by better transport links provided by the canals (see p. 21). However, for the workers, existence could be precarious. One of the brickfield workers who resided in North Hyde in 1881 was John Thorn.

South Lodge, The Green, c. 1901. The Lodge (built in the early to mid-nineteenth century) was at this time owned by Mr Richard Baxter (1856-1938), Chairman of the Southall-Norwood Urban District Council in 1903-1904 (see also p. 73) and resident at Featherstone Hall. An earlier resident, Major General William Paske of the Bengal Army, who was born in Madras, 1829, was one of the first men of Indian birth to have lived in Southall. Note The Three Tuns inn and the horse-drawn delivery vans on the right in the photograph.

Norwood Court, Norwood Green, c. 1900s. The house was probably built around 1800 and stood south of the Grand Junction Canal and to the west of Norwood Green. It possessed its own grounds and lake. Sydney Cole, a man of private means, and his family, lived here in 1891, with two live-in servants. It was demolished to make way for later housing developments.

Poplar Cottages, on the corner of King Street and Norwood Road, c. 1905. By 1914, R. White and Sons, mineral water manufacturers, had moved to South Road.

Townsend House, South Road (now Southall Broadway), c. 1905. William Hudson, a fifty-seven-year-old solicitor from Yorkshire, resided here in 1891, with his wife and two children and one domestic servant. The house itself was probably built in the late eighteenth century.

Sparrow Farm, North Road, *c.* 1925. The farm house dates from at least 1816. In 1851, Edmund Fairbrother was the head of the household. He was a farmer who farmed 66 acres and employed five labourers. By 1861 Fairbrother's son was no longer a farmer, but a cattle salesman.

Almshouses, North Road. These were constructed by William Deloitte (see p. 23) to mark Queen Victoria's Diamond Jubilee in 1897. Deloitte's widow, Mary Ann, donated £1,000 towards their endowment in 1898. They should not be confused with the almshouses near Norwood Green.

Grove House, North Road, July 1928. A house has been on this site since the eighteenth century (possibly 1740). John Warlow occupied the house when this picture was taken.

Gardens at The Chestnuts, The Green, c. 1930. The central figure is Mrs Percy Hume Hornby; the others are her three daughters, her son and her dog. They resided here from 1922 until 1932, when they left the district. Southall Hospital later stood on this site, the house being extended for that purpose. Note the library in the background (centre left).

The Cedars, Tentelow Lane, *c.* 1930s. This was a fine old Georgian mansion. In the early nineteenth century it was divided into two dwellings, the other being named Half House. There were seventeen rooms, two kitchens and three bathrooms. In 1963 it was rebuilt as an old people's home.

Rusticum Cottage, Norwood Green, 1946. Reputed to have been the oldest house in Southall, allegedly dating from 1580, it later became a garage, 'For all car services', both new and used, and for the sale of all motoring accessories. In 1946 it was pulled down.

The Chestnuts, Uxbridge Road, 1950. Built for Mr Stephen Walter Abbott (1863-1953) in 1904. He was the brother of Charles Thomas Abbott (see p. 60) and chairman of Abbott Brothers (Southall) Ltd, a local timber company, from 1929 to 1939.

Southall water tower, c. 1980. This forbidding and castle-like octagonal building was constructed in 1895 by the Hansons. It was 105ft tall it was called Southall's castle. Out of use by 1968, it was converted into six storeys of flats in 1984.

Three
Transport

Top Lock, Southall.

Norwood Top Lock in the early 1900s. This set of locks, and the cottages nearby, are so picturesque that they have attracted many artists to paint the view. Top Lock is the last of eleven locks up from the Thames.

Norwood Green Bridge, in the early 1900s. After the building of the canal, Norwood and Southall were separated by water; this bridge reunited them. Note the piping attached to the bridge.

The old bridge near the Grand Junction Arms, North Hyde, looking west, c. 1920. The farmhouse, possibly North Hyde Bridge Farm, on the left, was demolished shortly after this photograph was taken.

The new Wolf Bridge, 1925. The bridge takes Norwood Road across the Grand Union canal. Here we see the official weight testing of the bridge using heavy steam lorries, watched by a small crowd of boys and men.

The Grand Junction Canal, Southall, in the early 1900s. The canal was a great spur to economic development, allowing the brick fields to be properly exploited. Bricks could now be transported quickly and cheaply to Paddington. The canal was also used for pleasure cruises. Passengers could travel from Paddington to Uxbridge for 2s 6d between 1801 and 1853.

Southall railway station, 1890. The Great Western Railway first opened in Southall on 1 May 1839, but the station was little more than a hut by a level crossing until 1859. In 1880, single fares from Southall to Paddington were 1s 6d (first class) and 1s 2d (second class). In 1906 they were reduced to 1s 2d and 9d respectively. Railway buffs will note the broad and standard mixed-gauge tracks.

STATION. SOUTHALL.

Southall railway station and trains, c. 1910. The station building is in the centre of the background. About the station are goods ready to be transported; coal, milk and bricks. At this time, trains ran from Southall to Willesden Junction, Victoria and Brentford, as well as to Paddington. Note the water tower in the background.

Southall railway station entrance, *c.* 1954. Note that the sign for the station says, British Railways, denoting public ownership. Henry St John travelled by train to Kew, where he worked, and in 1933-1934, he conducted a one way romance with a young lady from Cowley. He wrote, despairingly, 'I first became aware of her when I began to travel from Southall to Kew. I have never spoken to her; she has said one word to me. That word was "Sorry" when she trod on my foot on a tram going from Kew Bridge to Brentford'.

Southall railway station, locomotive depot, *c.* 1960. Some of the last of the steam trains: they were finally withdrawn from service in December 1965.

Southall railway station, viewed from the east, looking west, 1961. This also shows one of the (then) new diesel railcars, the water tower and the gasworks in the background, though very few people.

Trumper's Crossing Halt, c. 1908. This was built to service the needs of Wyke Green and Osterley Park. It opened on 1 July 1904 and closed in 1926. The train is not a steam railcar but an auto-train, comprising a Wolverhampton class 0-6-0 T locomotive enclosed in a special body, hauling an auto-fitted trailer.

Three Bridges, *c.* 1910. This engineering masterpiece of 1859 by Isambard Kingdom Brunel is actually only two bridges for road (Windmill Lane) and the Grand Junction Canal. The railway, after all, does not need a bridge to travel on flat land. However, this coincidence of three modes of transport may be unique.

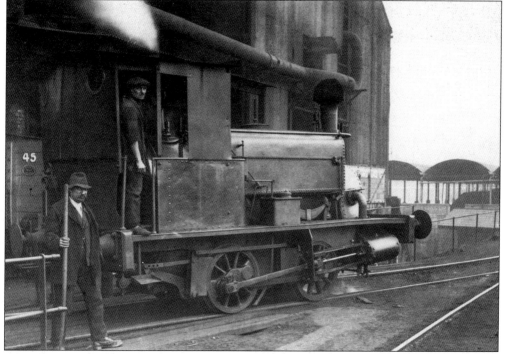

A shunting engine at the gasworks with a part of the Old Retort House before new installations of the 1920s. The gasworks in Southall was originally located in North Hyde between 1865-1868, but was then relocated to a site between the canal and the railway, just west of the railway station, having branches to both forms of transport. In 1910 their annual output was 18,000 million units.

Staff at Iron Bridge Service Depot, Iron Bridge, Uxbridge Road, celebrate Christmas in 1945. The service depot was founded in 1928 by Charles P. Abbott, who was also Deputy Charter Mayor (far right). It was a firm of motor engineers which repaired, amongst other vehicles, some of those produced by AEC.

Iron Bridge, 1950s. This bridge carried the railway over the Uxbridge Road. The first bridge burnt down in 1847 and the present bridge was built wholly of wrought iron. Note the AEC logo – a company which produced most of London's buses in Southall from 1927 to 1979 and which was based in Windmill Lane, not far from where this photograph was taken.

R. & G. Roe, removal contractors, Hambrough Road, *c.* 1890.

Horses and carts on the High Street, 1909. A very peaceful scene, with no trams operating at the time (but note the tram lines). There are three horse-drawn vehicles here – the third being mostly obscured by the gas lamp at the left of the view. The vehicle on the right is probably just coming back from having made a delivery to the Co-op on King Street.

The formal opening of the tram service, 10 July 1901. Although there had been plans for horse-drawn trams in 1871, to be run by the Southall, Ealing and Shepherd's Bush Tram Company, the line only ever reached Acton. The electric tramway was extended to Southall by 10 July 1901, by the London United Electric Tramways Company. There was a procession of five trams painted white and gold and decorated with roses. The town hall is decked out with flags and bunting to mark the event. A single fare to Shepherd's Bush cost three pence.

Tram on Southall Broadway, *c.* 1907. Note the town hall on the right of the picture. In 1904, the tramway was extended to Uxbridge. Trams were replaced in November 1936 by trolleybuses.

Open top tram on High Street, 1910. Motorised transport seems to have won the day. Apart from the tram, there is a motor car and a van. In the foreground, a pedestrian begins to make the perilous journey across the road.

Buses on King Street, 1954. Buses were a common sight in Southall from 1923 when the London General Omnibus Company and Cambrian began to run buses from London Bridge to Southall Town Hall. The first route number was 17B. Between the wars, there were twenty bus routes through Southall. From 1960, they were even more common as they replaced trolley buses in that year.

Cycles, lorries and cars on King Street, near Norwood Road, 1954.

"BRISTOL BIPLANE."
The First Flying Machine Landed in Southall 3rd July, 1911.

A Bristol Biplane in Southall, 3 July 1911. This plane was the first to land in Southall, at a field near Top Locks. Lieutenant Barrington-Kennett of the Coldstream Guards who was the airman, was taking part in the Standard Flying Race and had to land when his plane got into difficulties. On 5 July he was able to fly away to Hendon.

Four
Schools and Colleges

St Marylebone Schools, South Road, in the early 1900s. The school opened in 1858 for the poor children of the parish of St Marylebone, London. At that time there was a fashion for sending pauper children from unhealthy London to schools in more airy Middlesex – the more famous 'Cuckoo School' in Hanwell was another local example. During the First World War, the school was used as a hospital for wounded Australian soldiers.

Elisha Biscoe School, Tentelow Lane, Norwood Green, c. 1950. This was Southall's first school, founded in 1767 by Elisha Biscoe, who was steward to the Awsiter family, and a local landowner. Five years later he bequeathed £3,500 to pay a master and mistress to teach thirty-four local poor boys and girls. It was closed in 1950 and the house was sold to the last schoolmaster, Mr H. Vernall. Pupil registers from 1860-1950 are held at Ealing Library.

North Hyde Barracks, 1940s. A desolate end to St Mary's Catholic School for Boys. Six hundred poor boys whose parents were Catholic, attended this school, to be brought up in their parents' faith. The name barracks comes from the fact that prior to 1854, this had been an army barracks and it retained its military appearance.

'Three North Hyde School Heroes', 1915. During the first year of the First World War 234 old boys of the school joined the Army and 23 joined the Royal Navy. Many of those who joined the Army were bandsmen, which should be no surprise, since the school boasted a band, which had won many prizes in competitions. Many boys joined Irish regiments, too.

'Catholic cows going home', was the original caption for this picture, c. 1900. The name and whereabouts of the road are unknown. The cows had been milked and were returning to the North Hyde Barracks.

School picnic in Manor House Grounds, 1880s. The occasion and the school(s) involved are unknown. Clearly it was not a royal or national celebration; there are no flags. Presumably the children were local. It is possible that they were being treated by the kindly Thomases, who owned the Manor House at the time (p. 21).

Dudley Road Girls' School, c. 1900s. It opened in 1897, with three women teachers and eight classrooms. In 1900, the annual salary of Mrs Thompson, the headmistress, was raised from £100 to £120, due to the increasing numbers of pupils. By 1908, over four hundred girls attended, though this number was halved after 1918. In 1930 it became a junior mixed school.

Featherstone School, Featherstone Road, *c.* 1900. The school opened in 1890 and was initially a boys' school, with 200 scholars. Mr J. Dunn was the first headmaster. Its most famous pupil, who attended the school in the 1930s, was Cleo Laine, the jazz singer. She recalled, 'I liked the infant school as it was playtime rather than learning to me; I guess it was meant to prime one for the shock of going on to the higher school'.

Alec, Sylvia and Cleo Laine (born Clementina Dinah Hitchen in 1927). The three sisters learnt singing and dancing at Madame de Courcey's School of Dance, 41 Villiers Road, in the 1930s.

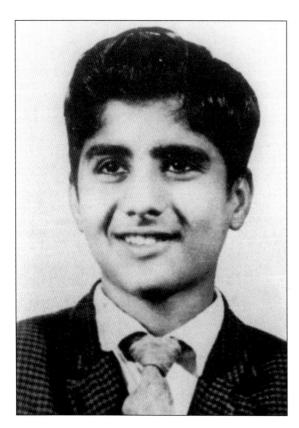

Resham Samra, a pupil at Featherstone Secondary High School, early 1962. At this time there were 380 school age children of immigrants in the borough. By 1967 forty-seven percent of the children who attended Featherstone School were of Asian descent.

The Clifton Road Schools were founded in 1904 and comprised infant and junior schools. This picture was probably taken not long after the schools were first opened. Note the Lipton van on the left. Lipton's, tea and provision merchants, had a branch on the Uxbridge Road, West Ealing.

Southall County School, in the 1920s. This was located in Villiers Road, and was described as, 'A Public Secondary School for Boys and Girls. It was founded in 1907. Initially, school fees were £2 2s 6d per term and it catered for children aged between eleven and fourteen. Each term consisted of thirteen weeks. School hours were from 9.00 until 4.15, except Wednesdays, Sundays and Saturday afternoons, which were free.

The Working Men's Club and Institute, 1906-1935, was eventually housed at 18 Featherstone Road (the house in the photograph is probably The Chestnuts, Southall Green). The premises were obtained by the members purchasing capital shares of five shillings each. It had a membership of 350. Such clubs provided social as well as educational amenities for working men. These were the sub-clubs; the athletics and the social. The highlight of the year was the annual dinner. Self-help, in the form of a Sick and Benevolent Society, was also promoted.

North Road Mixed Infants and Junior School, Class VIII, photographed in the early 1920s. The girls are apparently engaged in a domestic science lesson. This school had been founded in 1851 as a National School, but was largely demolished to make way for new buildings in 1915. At the time that this photograph was taken, Mr Jesse Payne was the headmaster and Mrs E. Dunn was the infant mistress.

A classroom scene at North Road School, c. 1963. After the Second World War, temporary accommodation was added to house the increasing numbers of children. Note the abacus and blackboard on the background.

Five
Public Services

Charter Day, 24 September 1936. The town was decorated with banners and bunting and there were events in Southall Park to mark the granting of the charter to Southall. These included sports, a historical pageant, tea for the old people and fireworks at ten o'clock. Between 10,000-20,000 people attended, more arriving as the day progressed. The local press observed, 'It was a wonderful spectacle'. It had all cost £773.

William Garrod, JP, Charter Mayor, greets guests on Charter Day, 1936. Born in 1882, Garrod had been a Southall resident since 1910. Since 1921 he had been a local Labour councillor. His first duty as charter mayor was to open a new stand at the football ground. His mace was presented by AEC, a local company, and his other regalia presented by other local groups and people, including Quaker Oats and the Earl of Jersey. Garrod died in 1960.

Grant of Arms, 1936. It had long been felt in civic circles that, though Southall had seen steady growth in population, industry and municipal life, and had achieved 'adult civic stature', it was 'still clothed as youth', being only the Southall-Norwood Urban District Council. Ealing had been incorporated in 1901 and Acton in 1921. A public enquiry was held and 250 pages of evidence were given promoting Southall for incorporation. Edward VIII duly granted the demand, but dropping Norwood from the borough's title offended some.

Town Hall, High Street, *c.* 1922. It was built in 1897 at a cost of £9,000, on land given by the district's most prominent landowner, the Earl of Jersey. It was built to honour the Diamond Jubilee of Queen Victoria and was opened by Lady Jersey on 8 November 1898.

The Council Chamber, 1949. From 1936, there were eighteen members, but by the 1950s, there were twenty-four. Each ward had three councillors and there were also six aldermen. At this time meetings were held on the fourth Tuesday of every month at seven o'clock. Charles P. Abbott, Chairman of Southall Independent Rate Payers' Association said, in October 1937, 'there was a dictatorship in our local affairs … as bad as in Germany'.

The town clerk's office, 7-9 South Road, 1955. The town clerk, until 1965, was the chief executive officer of the council. This building later became the Transport and General Workers' Union headquarters. The town clerk was usually a solicitor and also acted as the borough's legal adviser. In 1955 the post was held by Mr J. Syrett, who was appointed in 1947 and earned between £1,750 and £2,000 per annum.

Southall Library, Osterley Park Road, 1920s. This is a Carnegie Library, one of two in the modern London Borough of Ealing. The foundation stone was laid by Lady Jersey in 1904 and it was officially opened by Mrs Bigwood, wife of James Bigwood, MP, on 26 July 1905. It boasted a special section for industrial books and journals for students. On 4 June 1927, Henry St John sheltered here from the rain. He recorded that he read a copy of the journal *Labour Woman*, before noting his views on socialism, 'The Labour people are the most foolish and narrow minded in England'.

A library carnival float, raising public awareness of the borough's library service, photographed outside the library before a carnival procession in the early 1960s.

Opening of Jubilee Gardens Library, 28 May 1938. The mayor is Albert George Pargiter (1897-1982), who was thrice mayor of Southall. The two women are Alderman Mrs F.S. Amos, chairman (no politically correct 'chairs' then) of the Public Health Committee (left) and Mrs Dorothy Pargiter, the mayoress (left).

Jubilee Gardens Library at the time of its opening in 1938. This was 'a large modern Branch Library', 'conveniently planned and well equipped' to serve the northern part of the Borough. The cost of the library, together with that of the maternity and child welfare clinic built opposite, was £15,000.

The mayor also opened the Jubilee Gardens Health Clinic on 28 May 1938. This clinic provided maternity and child welfare services for the northern part of the borough. The name Jubilee Gardens refers to Jubilee Gardens Park, which was named to commemorate the Silver Jubilee of George V in 1935.

The Information Bureau, South Road, *c.* 1950. This was inaugurated in June 1948 and was open five days a week. It served to distribute council publicity, information about welfare services, accommodation and other matters. It claimed, 'The Information Bureau knows most things – what it does not know it will find out'. It clearly had international renown, as it was visited in April 1949 by Mr Short, a journalist from Sierra Leone. It later became the Red Cross Centre.

The town hall and fire station, 1930. The fire station, somewhat dwarfed by the town hall, was opened in 1901 and enlarged in 1904. Initially there was a chief officer, Harry Willis, a secretary and thirteen men. The first proper fire station cost £175. Charles Thomas Abbott (uncle of Charles P. Abbott) was the founder of the Volunteer Southall-Norwood Fire Brigade.

Christening the new fire engine on the Hamborough estate (owned by the Abbotts), 5 June 1901. It was named *Joan*, after the daughter of Charles Thomas Abbott, the first officer. She was present for the ceremony and is seen here standing with the new engine. Many of the firemen were also his employees. Abbott, who appears to have been popular with his men, died in 1905. He had many interests, both in business and leisure and was chairman of the council, 1899-1900 and 1904-1905.

Fire brigade out with the new engine. It was a Shand and Mason engine, of the Double Vehicle type, capable of pumping three hundred gallons per minute. One of the first major fires which it helped to extinguish was one at Otto Monsted's factory in December 1901.

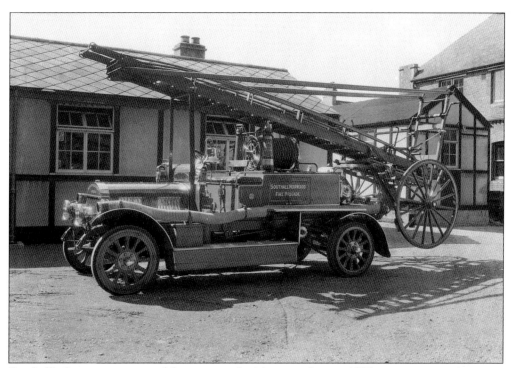

Southall's first motor-powered fire engine, the Merryweather, *c.* 1930.

Sir William Ellis, 1780-1839, first superintendent of the County Asylum and the first 'mental doctor' to be knighted for his services here. He was appointed as superintendent in 1831 and resigned in 1838, later living at Southall Park. His policy was that patients needed fresh air and exercise and that industry was therapeutic. Patients were put to work with spades, scythes and bill hooks and no accidents were recorded. Such treatment of the insane was revolutionary.

Dr John Conolly (1794-1866) was the third superintendent of the County Asylum and the most famous; he was appointed in 1839. Conolly's contribution was to build on the foundations laid by Ellis and to completely abandon the practice of patients being restrained by chains. Although this was not an original idea (the Quakers at York had advocated such in 1785) it was the first time it had been carried out in practice. By 1845, Conolly was in private practice, but was retained as the visiting physician.

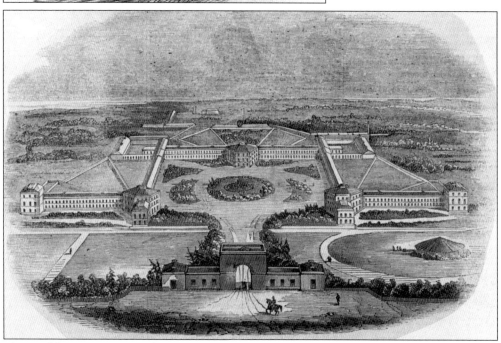

The Middlesex County Asylum was commonly known as the Hanwell Asylum since it was nearer to the village of Hanwell than to anywhere else. However, it was actually within the parish boundaries of Southall. In 1845 it was also referred to as the Southall Asylum. It did, however, serve the whole of the county.

Middlesex County Lunatic Asylum. The asylum was originally built in 1829-1831 for 300 patients. Over the years, the place was extended and by 1880, housed 2,000 patients. The Asylum was in many ways a self-contained village. Although the male staff wore uniforms, like goalers, they were also craftsmen whose job was to teach as much as to guard. Inmates would grow vegetables and work with tools to farm or make things. Goods were delivered to and from the asylum partly by canal, for there was an asylum docks connected to the Grand Junction Canal.

Later the asylum became the London County Asylum following its taking over by London County Council in 1889. In 1937 it was known as St Bernard's Hospital and today is part of Ealing Hospital. Here are the staff members who doubled as the fire brigade for the asylum. The brigade was formed in 1873 from existing staff who received extra pay for the responsibility.

Dr George Bruce McDonald, 1890s. Born in Perth in 1842, he had a general practice at Denmark Road and did his rounds on a tricycle. In 1896 he was joined in his practice by Dr Jabez Windle. McDonald was also the Medical Officer for the Norwood District of the Uxbridge Union. He was a tall man and wore a bowler hat. It was said that he had two sides to his character depending on whether his patient was one of the good payers, or not. McDonald resided at No. 8 Alexandra Villas, Western Road with his family and four servants. He also wrote the preface to Samuel Short's *Southall and its Environs* of 1910.

Mr Green's dental surgery, No. 95 South Road, *c.* 1931. In 1910, Mr Green boasted that, 'He will save you pain. His charges are moderate. He will also save you money'. Three dentists with the name of Green worked from this address in the 1920s and 1930s; E.H. Green, from 1922-1923, Algernon Earnest Green in 1925 and Ernest Herbert Green from 1926. The latter had a telephone installed in about 1931.

The post office in South Road, c. 1950. Until about 1845, The Red Lion served as Southall's posting house, alongside the official post office. By 1887 the post office was on the corner of Featherstone Road and Featherstone Terrace. The one here had entrances in both South Road and Beaconsfield Road. It opened in July 1938 and was described as having been designed in 'a free rendering of traditional Georgian'.

The police hut, North Road, c. 1910. In 1914, one sergeant Charles Hudson was in charge. At this time, the local police was part of the T division of the Metropolitan Police. By 1917, there was a total of nineteen officers serving the district.

The municipal piggeries, at the former Wyke Green Sewage Works by the Brent, c. 1950. These were established in 1940, with fourteen pigs, to help deal with the national food shortage caused by war. Although they ran at a loss, and there were calls to sell them off, they remained until 1960. Here is the pedigree boar, Ted.

'Pride in his work'. A young lad helps care for the council pigs, c. 1950. This, and the preceding photograph, featured in a book of pictures of the piggeries which, it is thought, was prepared to support a case for keeping them in council control, rather than selling them off, as the Conservative opposition on the council at the time proposed.

66

Six
Religion

St Mary's, Tentelow Lane, Norwood Green, *c.* 1807. Since 1859 this was the parish church of Norwood, previously it had been a chapel of ease for Hayes. There has been a church on this site since the time of the Normans and possibly even earlier. The oldest parts of the present building date from the twelfth to the early fifteenth centuries. Henry Chichele, Archbishop of Canterbury (1414-1443), and lord of the manor, was involved with the rebuilding.

The fifteenth-century font at St Mary's which was given by Archbishop Chichele. Elsewhere in the church are reminders of worthy local residents; there is an effigy of John Merrick, who died in 1749, and a brass to Francis Awsiter, who lived in the Manor House and died in 1624.

St John's old church, King Street, Southall Green, the parish church of Southall. This was endowed and built in 1837-1838 with money given by Henry Dobbs (or Dodds as he is sometimes called), owner of the Southall vitriol factory. The church was consecrated in 1841 and was later used as a church hall.

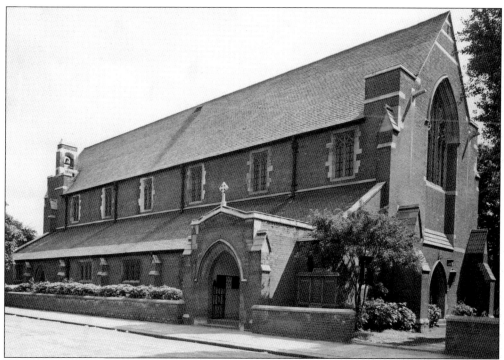

St John's new church, Church Avenue. By 1910 the old church was too small for its congregation. C.G. Miller built the new building on the grounds that had once belonged to Elmfield House. A tablet in the new church commemorates the benefactor of the old church. Ernest Ham (1874-1958), a prolific painter of scenes of old Southall, was a regular worshipper here.

Interior, St John's new church, c. 1910.

St John's vicarage, Southall Green, *c.* 1890. This is a copy of a painting by Ernest Ham, a local artist. The vicarage stood opposite the old church. In 1891, the vicar was the Revd John Jackson, who resided here with his wife and two servants.

The original iron church, Holy Trinity, Uxbridge Road, which opened on 15 November 1868. This, Southall's third church, was moved from Brentford and reassembled at Southall at a cost of £200. It was built in Mr Bignell's field, opposite The Three Horse Shoes and the Revd W.E. Littlewood was the first vicar.

Holy Trinity church, Uxbridge Road, c. 1900. By the end of the 1880s the old iron church, having withstood the weather of years at both Brentford and Southall, was beginning to be less than rain proof. In 1887 there was a meeting which resolved to build a permanent church at the end of what is now Park View Road on land given by the Earl of Jersey. It was built by John Lee in 1890 and opened on 31 January 1891.

Holy Trinity church parish hall, Lady Margaret's Road, c. 1910. By 1976, rotting timbers had forced the hall to close and later it was sold to pay for a new and smaller hall. This hall was later converted into the Vishwa Hindu Kendra.

Holy Trinity church interior.

A League of Mercy garden party, held at Richard Baxter's house, South Lodge, in August 1908. Baxter was vice-president of this organisation and the event was to raise funds for the League of Mercy and Good Samaritan League. Four thousand people attended and £100 was raised, to be split between the two charities. The sporting highlight was a three-mile marathon through the town and the winner was Mr H. Broome. He was awarded a silver watch and chain. There were also children's races.

Havelock Road cemetery, *c.* 1950s. Named after Sir Henry Havelock, a hero of the Indian Mutiny. The cemetery was opened in 1883 as local churchyards became too crowded. It was consecrated by the Bishop of London in the same year. In 1924 the grounds were extended. In the background can be seen St John's church and the gas holder.

The cemetery chapel. This small chapel and the mortuary were built in 1896 and 1895 respectively. Both have subsequently been pulled down

The tithe barn, Southall Green, *c.* 1900. The building dates from the early seventeenth century and was part of the manor house's property. Francis Awsiter allowed a Catholic priest from St Anselm's, Hayes, to hold Mass here, prior to the building of St Anslem's church in 1906. The hall was also used for social events. It was pulled down in 1915.

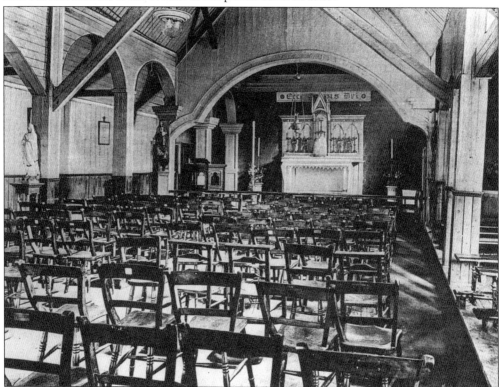

Inside the tithe barn, during its period as a Catholic church, *c.* 1910.

Wesley Hall, Cambridge Road, *c.* 1885. There was a Wesleyan chapel here from at least 1865; the first non-conformist chapel to be built in Southall. It was de-registered in 1907.

King's Hall, Wesleyan Methodist chapel, South Road, 1950. The occasion is the 18th Festival of Young People, held on 13 May. The chapel itself was built in 1916 and Sir Alfred Gelder of Hull was the architect. It is an imposing three-storey building and the centre for Methodism in the district.

Number 11 Beaconsfield Road was used as a Sikh temple in 1962, the first Sikh temple in Southall. The house was bought on behalf of the committee in 1961. Mr Hukham Singh (centre) was the Speaker of the Indian Parliament at the time. The premises proved too small and a larger site was acquired on Southall Green in 1965.

A scene at the birthday celebration for Guru Nanak Dev ji at Featherstone Road school hall in 1962. Guru Nanak Dev ji, born in 1469 and the founder of Sikhism, is always depicted as holding his palm upwards towards the viewer in a gesture of blessing and peace. Mr Surjit Singh Bilga addressed the gathering.

Seven

War and Peace

Southall Special Constabulary, September 1917. Special constables were called up during times of war or civil emergency and disbanded once the crisis was over. They supplemented the work of the regular police, many of whom had enlisted with the colours at this time. The regular police did not think them to be particularly efficient!

The Maypole Institute and Otto Monsted Hospital, viewed from the east, c. 1916. The Maypole Institute was built for the employees of the Otto Monsted Works and became a military hospital in 1915. Note the Australian headgear on two of the men. The Institute was used as an ARP canteen and recreation room during the Second World War.

The games room in the Otto Monsted Hospital, c. 1916. Note the three Boy Scouts watching the game of miniature billiards in progress. Music, draughts and reading were among the pastimes available.

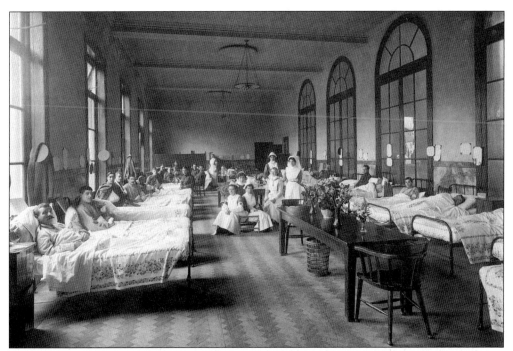

A hospital ward in the Otto Monsted Hospital, c. 1916.

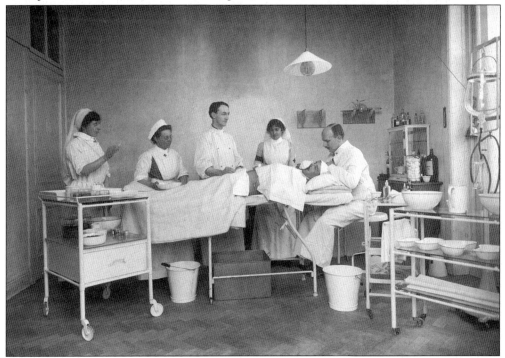

A treatment room in the Otto Monsted Hospital, c. 1916. Dr Chill was in charge and had eleven general auxilliary nurses to assist him. In total they helped 3,300 patients, of whom only four died in their care. 2,520 patients were from France. On 23 November 1916, the hospital was visited by King George V and Queen Mary. There were 102 patients there at the time.

Southall war memorial, with Remembrace Day wreaths, in the 1920s. Of the 3,500 men of Southall who served in the First World War, 800 were killed. Some of the names of the men who fought can be found in the Memorial Book, composed in 1915. A copy is held at Ealing Library. The memorial in the picture was designed with the Cenotaph in Whitehall in mind.

Southall war memorial, Armistice Day, 1920s. The memorial was unveiled on 8 April 1922 by Colonel Sidney Peel, DSO, MP for Uxbridge (Southall did not become a Parliamentary constituency in its own right until 1945).

A page from the Southall and Norwood Roll of Honour, 1915. This was published by John King, printer, and listed names, addresses and other details of Southall men who had volunteered for the fighting services between 1914-1915. It was to record 'the part that Southall played by its magnificent contribution of men to His Majesty's Forces in the Great European War'.

The unveiling of the Featherstone Road School war memorial, on 16 February 1921 by Sir William Robinson. The memorial, to commemorate the Old Boys and masters who had perished in the conflict. It was a bronze statue of a soldier. Sadly, the monument was stolen in 1982.

The town hall, *c.* 1939. Note the sandbags to the left of the Town Hall. These were first placed here during the Munich crisis of 1938 when war was felt to be imminent. Other public buildings were similarly protected.

Loading up the guns for salvage, 1940. Three German field guns were presented to the Southall British Legion in 1919 by the Australian Government and were salvaged as scrap metal for munitions. The local press remarked on the occasion that the guns were to 'pass into the fight for the preservation of freedom and justice'.

War Weapons Week, 18 May 1941. This procession down the Uxbridge Road was part of a drive to raise public awareness and collect money to help the war effort. At this time, neither the USSR nor the USA had yet joined the British Empire's war effort. Here the ARP sections and a model bomb can be seen.

War Weapons Week, May 1941. The mayor, Alderman F.G. Smith, passes through a guard of honour formed by the Home Guard from the Gas, Light and Coke Company, when he attended the company's showrooms, No. 32 South Road, to receive cheques and tokens of investments from local firms and organisations. In all, £4,613 11s was raised here.

War Weapons Week, May 1941. The mayor, standing, is seen here at Tudor Road school, another selling centre for savings stamps and certificates. Seated is the supervisor, Mr W.H. Barnes. The sum of £1,220 12s 6d was raised at the school.

Wartime Salvage Drive, 14 September 1941. A procession through the streets of the town, eventually reaching Southall Park, was devised to draw attention to the town's salvage effort. The tricyclist is Mr G.T. Robinson, the 'King of Salvage', wearing old clothing decorated with bits of salvage. Behind him are the 'Knights of Salvage'.

Wartime Salvage Drive, September 1941. The ladies of the Norwood Townswomen's Guild at Norwood Green, with bags of salvage which had been collected. The tableau which they created had trays showing different kinds of salvage. The salvaged materials, of course, went to make munitions for war use. Southall's salvage drive collected 94 tons of salvage in three days.

The construction of an emergency water tank in Manor Gardens, March 1943. There were comments in the local press about its adverse effect on the aesthetic beauty of the Manor House grounds, but these had to be endured because of wartime necessity, as Alderman George Pargiter observed.

A Southall stretcher party, possibly at Norwood Green, May 1941. The gentleman inspecting the men may be Lt. Colonel John Llewellin, MP for the Uxbridge division, which included Southall.

The rescue and ambulance station, Salisbury Road, c. 1942. Fortunately, the number of raids on Southall were few, even compared to Ealing which was itself far less damaged than some parts of London. Even so, 126 high explosive bombs, hundreds of incendiary bombs and 7 V1 rockets fell on the town, causing 255 casualties, of which 22 were fatal.

The rescue and ambulance station, Salisbury Road, staff canteen. The workers take a well-earned break. A food cupboard in the canteen was only added in 1943.

Borough Café No. 4 at 233-235 Allenby Road. This and other Borough Cafés were run by the council to provide reasonably priced meals. Borough Cafés, sometimes known as British Restaurants, served midday meals that could help supplement rations. Some meals were take-away only. This one opened in 1942 but was decommissioned in November 1943 because it had been running at a heavy loss. According to Alderman Pargiter, this was because it was badly sited.

A Civil Defence sergeant in the doorway of a shelter on the junction between Rutland Road and Somerset Road, 1943. Street shelters of this kind were to shelter those caught in the open during air raids, especially those for which there was usually little or no warning, as with the V1 rockets in 1944. One was needed here because it was on a route used by hundreds of war workers. After the war these eyesores were removed, though not until early 1946.

Building of the Dormers Wells Housing estate, July 1945. The man with the spade in front of the excavator is a German prisoner of war. The cap was part of the German Army uniform. Many POWs remained in England for some time after the war as cheap labour, though given the scarcity of food in Germany, this was probably a blessing in disguise.

This a VE Day (Victory in Europe) children's street party, 8 May 1945 in Spike's Bridge Road. The mayor is Councillor Frederick J. Marks. It was observed that many of the younger children here would never have known what a party was until this one. Such celebrations were not always popular. On 9 May, Henry St John wrote, 'a party in a nearby house went on until 2 a.m., with music, dancing, singing and shouting, so I could not sleep until well past that hour … I felt good for nothing today'.

One of the VE Day street processions with one man in drag and another with a blacked face, 9 May 1945. This one was for the children of Lea and Williams Road. According to the local press, the procession was 'headed by the local comics and clowns'. Afterwards they went to Messrs H.G. Sanders and Sons' staff canteen for a 'bumper tea'. In the evening there were games in Lea Road.

A Victory tea party, 19 September 1945, for the children of St Peter's Road and Cornwall Avenue. Presumably this was to celebrate VJ Day (Victory over Japan) on 15 August following VE Day on 8 May.

The Armistice Parade, with men and boys of the uniformed services marching up Southall Green, 11 November 1950. The procession included the pipe band of the local Air Training Corps and a detachment from the United Service Corps on their first public appearance in England. Note the Century cinema in the background. At this time, British troops were serving in the Korean War.

Eight

Work

NORWOOD MILL.

Norwood Flour Mill, situated on the north bank of the Grand Junction Canal, west of the
Norwood Road in 1912. There had been a steam flour mill here since the 1860s. In 1906
George Haigh used the place to make plaster moulds and picture frames. After the 1960s, it
became a council childcare building. Note Wolf Bridge to the centre of the picture.

1899 to Harry who worked in the gardens

The flour mill burnt down long before the 1960's
My granny Ada Parslow was a maid to the owners
of the flour mill before her marriage in

The Market Charter, 1698. Southall cattle market was founded by a charter of 11 November 1698, granted by William III (pictured in the left hand corner of the charter) to Francis Merrick, a local landowner (coincidentally, both died in 1702). The charter gave permission for a cattle market to be held in Southall on Wednesdays and for two fairs to be held annually. The charter is in Latin.

Southall Cattle Market in 1949. By 1806 there were three acres of land allocated for the market and it was claimed that the amount of business done there was so large that it was second only to Smithfield. However, in the middle of the nineteenth century, the market was in decline, but by 1929 there had been a slight revival. The market was then the only livestock and poultry market in the county, though it was also a general retail and stall market, too. In 2001 the market still exists, but has changed out of all recognition. The Red Lion can be seen in the background.

Old Market House, No. 50 High Street, 1928. This was the house where the auctioneer and his family lived. In the 1910s, auctions began at 11.30 a.m. Henry Elliot was the auctioneer and had been so since 1925.

The Martin Brothers' pottery, Havelock Road in 1895, taken from a painting by Ernest Ham. After originally working in Fulham, the brothers moved to Southall in 1877 and took over an old soap factory as their pottery. They produced over 500 items in a good year. However, as the brothers began to grow older, less work was done and virtually none after 1915. The pottery burnt to the ground in 1946 and a housing estate now stands on the site.

The canal was used to bring in the clay.

Three of the Martin Brothers, Walter, Wallace and Edwin, during the 1890s, at work on the Wally Birds. The Martin Brothers have been called 'Southall's most distinguished citizens'. There were four of them, Charles (1846-1910), Walter (1859-1912), Edwin (1860-1915) and Robert Wallace (1844-1923). Between them they sculpted thousands of salt glazed stoneware items, known collectively as Martinware. These were sculpted with humurous and imaginative images, often quite ugly, such as the Wally Birds (pictured).

Edwin Martin at work. He was often the decorator of Martinware. He had no professional training and was self taught. Although he did work for a time at Doulton's in Lambeth, he is said to have done many of the jobs that no one else wanted.

Walter Martin at work on the potter's wheel. Walter produced classical and oriental style vases. He also made stoneware items. During his ten-year courtship of Rose Thornecroft, he gave her gifts of stoneware scent bottles. Despite this attention the romance came to an end in 1895.

An unnamed girl in the allotment gardens, with the Martins' kiln in background, c. 1924. Note the rural surroundings.

Home Farm, viewed from the barn. Home Farm was situated on the westside of the Green, just north of South Lodge. It had existed since at least 1816 and possessed orchards to the north of the farm buildings and just south of the railway. In 1891 it was just known as The Farm, and was inhabited by Henry Phelps Baxter and his family (see p. 23).

Offices of Otto Monsted Ld, Southall. W3199.

The Otto Monsted margarine factory offices, c. 1900. The factory was built in 1893-1894 and opened in 1895. Otto Monsted was a Dane and in its day the factory was the largest margarine works in the country. The factory was well sited, with its own railway sidings and a branch of the canal.

Production workers on the shop floor at the Otto Monsted factory, c. 1910. The works, which employed hundreds of local people, was a model factory. The air conditioning, hygiene standards and the staff welfare facilities were excellent. There was a works club, later called the Maypole Institute, where workers could eat and drink, play billiards or read in the library. This was built in 1910 by the Hansons at a cost of £13,850. The factory closed in 1929.

Women workers at the factory, c. 1916. During the First World War, with men volunteering and later being conscripted to fight, many more women, especially the wives of servicemen, began to work in this and other factories. On 28 March 1917, the chairman observed, 'Practically all the eligible men at the distributing stores have joined the Army and have been replaced by the employment of over 2,000 females. Wherever practicable, female labour is also used in the Works'. Of the 463 factory workers who fought, 52 were killed.

Men at work on The Green, demolishing the wall of South Lodge to allow widening of the road, c. 1910. Compare the photograph on page 27.

The opening of the Southall and Norwood sewage works with staff and local councillors present, 28 July 1903. The works were opened by Sir Ralph Littler, chairman of the Middlesex County Council. Also in the group are Reginald Brown, Southall Council's Engineer from 1901-1919. and Charles Jones, Ealing's Surveyor (back row, eighth from the left).

The sewage works was near the Grand Junction Canal opposite the Hanwell sewage works. The total cost of construction was £8,750. The council was obliged to spend this money following litigation with Middlesex County Council over pollution of the Brent.

Gibson's Yard next to the Palace Cinema in South Road, 1928. During this year, the yard was used by D.J. Kirby, builder, Joseph Albert Tregellis, motor engineer and Edwards and Thomson, auctioneers.

Southall and Norwood refuse and incineration plant, Adelaide depot, 1932. On the south, the plant bordered the Grand Union Canal and on the east, Norwood Mill. The plant cost £13,422 and the engineer was Mr J.B. Thomson. There were complaints by Norwood residents in 1936 because of the fumes it emitted. It was opened on 28 September 1932 by the chairman of the council, Mr James Albert Saxon.

The rubber factory of R. Woolf and Co., Hayes Bridge, 1951. This building had previously been a tyre factory, built in the 1930s. It resembles, on a far smaller scale, the more famous Art Deco Hoover building at Perivale. Woolf's opened here in 1951 and in the early 1950s, part of its workforce was made up of newly arrived Indian workers, most of whom worked as labourers. By 1960, forty percent of Sikh men living in Southall worked here.

Vishnu Sharma (front row, far left), under-secretary of the Indian Workers' Association (IWA), with a group of fellow workers, photographed in a Southall garden, c. 1958. The organisation was founded on 3 March 1957 to safeguard the interests of the newly arrived Indian workers. The group is all male which is perhaps not surprising since, at this time the 1961 census shows that 1,200 male Indians were resident but only 478 women. This was usual – families arrived later after the men had found work.

Meeting at the Community Centre, Merrick Road, October 1958. Pictured on the far left is Mr A.S. Takher, President of the newly formed IWA, on his right is Mr Jaswant Singh Dhami, Acting President of the IWA. On his right is Mr L. Fletcher, district manager of ABC Cinemas and behind him, Mr J.H. Smith, manager of the Dominion. Mr Takher was about to leave for India. The occasion is a meeting between IWA members and local trades unionists to create closer ties between the two groups.

George Pargiter, MP for Southall, 1950-1966, (centre) addressing a meeting at the Dominion in 1962 on the subject of the new Immigration Act. On the left are Claudia Jones, an American activist, and Jaswant Dhami, President of the IWA. On the far right is Vishnu Sharma, Under-Secretary of the IWA.

Southall gasholder, 1960s. This view of part of the gasworks is from the railway station bridge. It lies to the west of the railway station. In 1958, the annual output of gas was 5,932 million cubic feet, which entailed the consumption of 4.5 million gallons of oil annually

My friends father – June Lew Charles was a chemist there

Nine
Shopping

Harewood Place, Norwood Green, *c.* 1950. The two shops here, Nos 1 and 2, had been grocers and confectioners for many years. John Henry Maw, grocer, had been there since at least 1914, while Poole moved there in 1930, taking over from a previous confectioner.

Always Known as Maws Corner.

Industrial and Co-operative Stores, Nos 2-4 King Street, *c.* 1895. In 1914 Robert Whitticar was the manager. Previously, the town stocks had stood on this site. Another branch of the store opened at Nos 28-30 King Street in 1937, in the space left by a burnt out drapery shop run by Endacott's.

London Co-operative Society Ltd, Nos 2-4 King Street, *c.* 1950. The same shop as above, only renamed and half a century later. Note the changes to the shop front and to the windows, as well as to the road and the transport. In 1956, there were thirteen Co-op stores in Southall.

King Street, *c*. 1914. Edwin James Quinion, furniture dealers, had the premises at No. 60 King Street, and, from 1926, another shop at No. 66, previously owned by S.A. and E. Garlands, also furniture dealers.

Harry Frederick Hardy's hair cutting and shaving saloon, No. 47 King Street, *c*. 1910. By 1914 Hardy referred to himself as a 'hairdresser' and by 1930 had moved to No. 55 King Street. A year later he had evidently taken his son into the business for it became Hardy and Son.

Frank Camble Loaring and Sons, ironmongers and hardware store, No. 34 King Street, 1920s. A paint, enamel and varnish display was featured outside the shop on this day. Loaring's shop was here from at least 1914 until around 1980.

A parade of shops at Nos 67-73 King Street seen in 1954. Note the Sunshine Library, surely one of the last of the private libraries in Southall. Nos 71 and 73 had been a confectioner's and a butcher's, though in different hands, in the 1930s. However Charles Payne and Henry Foster had survived from that decade.

Francis' furniture shop, Sketchleys drycleaning and Lesley's newsagents, Nos 59-63 King Street, c. 1955. These businesses were all established after 1945. Lesley's had replaced Fred Slatter, tobacconist.

Thomas R. Langler, the baker's, High Street, c. 1895. Presumably the lady in the picture is Mrs Langler. There was another Langler, a draper (a possible relation?) in the High Street at the time. In 1885, an advertisement for the Langler's seen here read, 'Everything of the very best Quality, and at the Lowest Cash Prices. Celebrated for Cakes and Gingerbread. Biscuits of all Best Kinds in Stock.'

Langler's the drapers and West's the corn dealers, High Street, opposite Avenue Road, *c.* 1900. The Langler women had been linen drapers on the High Street since at least 1881 and continued until 1917, probably giving up due to old age; the youngest, Mary Ann Langler was sixty-two in 1917. John West, baker, was born in Southall in 1816 and started the business which was continued by his son, Thomas Bentall West, who was also a coal dealer.

High Street, *c.* 1910. The drapers on the left of the picture is probably that of George Clifton Brown's. He had premises at Nos 20-26 High Street. Note the different forms of transport on view.

William Quinion's saddle and harness-makers shop at No. 57 High Street and the White Hart inn, 1928. The Quinion family had been saddlers in Southall since at least 1885. Frederick Cork Quinion, born 1837 had been the first in the business. His grandson, also F.C. Quinion, was still trading as a saddler in 1930. Note the Victorian post box in the foreground.

High Street and Broadway at the junction with Lady Margaret Road, c. 1960. H.J. Butler and Co., the tailors and outfitters, had premises at Nos 1-3 The Broadway from 1928. The shop was established in about 1905 and was still going strong in the 1950s. They were boys' clothiers as well as tailors to adults. They advertised that they had the 'Expert services of Cutters and Workmen on the premises'.

My father & Grand Father shopped at Butlers. Also a barbers. The "magic" scissors an illuminated sign which moved was loved by all at the top on

H.J. Butler's, Nos 7-9 The Broadway, 1915. During the First World War, many of the men who worked in the shop joined up. The shop's patriotic announcement ran, 'Our Establishments are Landmarks well known to most of our brave Southall Men who have responded to the call of King and Country'. J. Scott (inset) was apparently the shop's manager.

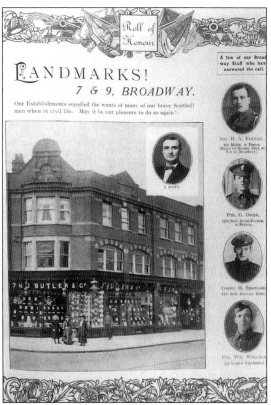

Haddrell House, on the corner of the Uxbridge Road and Herbert Road, *c.* 1956. Rebuilt in 1930 this was the largest furniture store in Southall. William Hadrell Ltd had occupied Nos. 29-33 Broadway since 1914. According to their advertisement of 1922, they sold linoleum, carpets, rugs, curtains and stored furniture. They were called the 'Complete House FURNISHERS'.

Southall Broadway, c. 1942. Despite the generally peaceful appearance, this photograph was taken during the Second World War; notice the advertisement for Victory Savings Bonds on the bank. Southall, like most parts of Britain in 1942 and 1943, was relatively free from bombing raids. The Luftwaffe during this period concentrated its attention on the Soviet Union. In 1931, Henry St John made two observations about Southall Broadway. On 7 June, he noted, 'A woman was standing on the shady south side of the Broadway selling matches.' On Christmas Day he made a cryptic reference to 'Southall's vice arcade' on the Broadway but there was no indication as to why he felt he should have been so disparaging about it!

South Road, looking south, December 1936. Note the Palace Cinema on the right. There are some new shop premises on the left and there were still more to come.

Butler's the tailors, on the junction of South Road and the Uxbridge Road, *c.* 1949. On 26 February 1942, Henry St John noted, 'At Butlers' (3.36 p.m.) I ordered a brown suit, price £7 10s, with 17s 6d purchase tax. I have never had a suit at such an enhanced price. The shopman said it was correct that only 15% of wool was allotted for civilian needs. In the last war it was 20%. It had been increasingly hard to get the heavier wool cloths.'

North Road, *c.* 1950. Note the horse-drawn delivery van still in use. Such vans gradually became less common after 1950. In the war years, very few motor vehicles were made for civilian use. That and petrol rationing until 1950 brought the mechanisation of light delivery services to a halt for almost ten years; indeed the trend was reversed and horsepower was relied on instead.

Ten

Leisure

Norwood Green, 1950s. Spectators watch a cricket match on a summer's day. This is possibly the Norwood Green Cricket Club which has been in existence since 1876. The Green covered about seven acres and was bordered with Elms.

Beating the bounds, 28 March 1927. This picture was taken on the parish boundary between Southall-Norwood parish and Hanwell parish, on Hanwell bridge over the Brent which conveniently marks the boundary. Beating the bounds was an ancient custom to remind parishioners, in years before maps, where the boundary of the parish was. The willow wands carried here were used to beat the boundary marks, or in early days, the boys who accompanied the adults. Visits to a few public houses were usually included in the route on these jolly occasions.

Another view of the boundary beaters, walking along the Brent, headed by the local constable. Originally the constable was a parish official, so his presence here is another reminder of antiquity. Note the schoolmaster bringing up the rear. In the 1870s, parish officials were given expenses for beating the bounds – perhaps for beer money.

The Three Horse Shoes, High Street, *c.* 1900. This is the original building, which was built in the 1850s, seen shortly before it was demolished to make way for the present structure.

The White Hart, High Street, *c.* 1930. The pub had a special licence for Wednesday mornings until 3.00 a.m. to be able serve the customers at the cattle market opposite. Originally it had been a coaching inn. Thomas William Judge was the publican in 1930. It was rebuilt in 1934. The rock band, The Who, (Daltrey, Entwistle, Townshend and Moon), played one of their first concerts here on 6 August 1964.

The Red Lion, High Street, *c.* 1930. James E.C. Carr was the proprietor of the 'hotel', as this other High Street pub liked to call itself, in 1930. Note the advertised Tea Gardens, doubtless added to give the establishment added class. A public house of this name had existed on the High Street since at least the mid-seventeenth century.

Southall Tennis Club, 1900s. Founded in 1898 as Southall Lawn Tennis and Croquet Club, it had its headquarters at Park View, High Street and in 1914 its honorary secretary was Shapland Abbott. Charles Thomas Abbott had helped to found the club in the 1890s.

Southall Ramblers Cycling Club, 1905. The club had been resuscitated in this year, and had organised twenty-one cycle runs and three or four 'ladies' runs'. In October their annual concert was held at the Berkeley Arms, Cranford. Note the cycles held by the lads on the right and left of the main group. The club does not seem to have been long lived – they are not mentioned in the 1914 local directory.

Western Road football ground, c. 1950. The ground opened on 17 September 1905 with a crowd of 300. This was the home ground of Southall Football Club (founded 1871) which merged with Southall Athletic in 1906. According to one local report, 'Improvements carried out at this ground have made it one of the first of its type in the country'. The club had its finest hour in 1925, when it was beaten 2-1 by Clapton at the final of the Amateur Cup, played at New Cross.

London County Council Asylum against Middlesex County Cricket Team (Amateurs, or Mr G.W. Beldam's XI), 8 July 1909. The most famous English cricketer of all time, Dr W.G. Grace (1848-1915), is seated in the centre. He only played twice in the 1909 season and on this occasion he only made three runs. Although he briefly resided in Leamington Road, Acton, he had no other local connection. The game actually took place in Hanwell. The Asylum Team won by 163 runs to 136.

The Gem, or The Southall Electric Cinema, the Green, 1938. This was Southall's first cinema and it opened in 1910. The original building had a mock-Elizabethan façade. In 1917 the cinema showed films of current tank warfare, taken on the Western Front. It was rebuilt in 1929 and later re-named The Century. It closed in 1957 and was reopened to show Indian films.

The Paragon Palace 'Cinematograph Theatre' South Road, 1927. Opened in 1912, it was built by A. & B. Hanson with 300 tip-up seats and held penny matinees on Saturday afternoons. *The Black Diamond Express* was then showing, a Warner Brothers film starring Monty Blue and Claire McDowell. Note that the timbered building to the left of the cinema was due for demolition in order that a 'super cinema' be erected there.

Palace Cinema, (later The Godina and even later, The Liberty), South Road, 1929. This was built on the site of The Paragon Palace by A & B Hanson Ltd. Note the Chinese-style exterior. The film *Blackmail*, then showing, was one of Alfred Hitchcock's early films. It is now a listed building. Henry St John visited the cinema on 7 August 1937 with his aunt and uncle to watch *The Little Princess*, starring Shirley Temple. They had intended to patronize the Odeon, but there were no seats there under 1s 6d! The cinema was used as an indoor market by the 1970s.

Site of the Dominion Cinema, The Green, early 1930s. Yet again, the Hansons were the builders. The Dominion was opened on 14 October 1935 by the famous Lancastrian actress Gracie Fields. It originally boasted a large organ, a ballroom and a cafeteria. The three people deep in conversation are Mrs Trump, Lucy Ayres, later Trump, and Thomas Whitehouse.

The Dominion Cinema, 1935. This looks indeed to be the super cinema that was promised in the posters. This was the heyday of Shirley Temple and of such classic films of Empire such as *Sanders of the River*. It closed in 1962 and re-opened to show Indian films.

Southall Bowl, formerly The Odeon, High Street, *c.* 1960s. The Odeon was opened in August 1936 by the last ever Chairman of the Southall Norwood Urban District Council, Mr Ernest Hamblin. The façade of this building was 'a modern interpretation of a classical treatment'. When the cinema closed in 1961, the building was used first as a bowling alley and then as a fittings stores.

Southall boy scouts outside the public library in 1910. Scouting had only begun three years before when Sir Robert Baden Powell had held the Brownsea Island experiment. This troop may have been Lady Jersey's Own, the First Norwood. Mr Jubb was the scoutmaster and Arthur Collins his assistant (far right).

Entrance to Southall recreation grounds, 1908. Note the lodge and the bandstand in the background. The eighteen acres of land on which the recreation ground was formed was originally known as Bill's Charity Land. It was bought by the council in 1902 and became a public park a year later. In 1906 the bandstand, offices and lodge were built.

The lake, Southall Park, c. 1923. The park, the largest in Southall, covered twenty-six acres and was purchased by the council in 1909. The lake was constructed in 1922. The park stands on what were the grounds of Dr Robert Boyd's private asylum which burned down on 14 August 1883 with the loss of six lives, including that of Dr Boyd.

Southall Park bandstand, c. 1910. This must have seemed a rural idyll for the little children in the centre. Musical programmes were a regular feature on Sunday evenings in summer.

The Horticultural Exhibition in Southall Park, 24-25 August 1946. The mayor, standing on the left, (with barely concealed cigarette) is Frederick Earnest Gardner. Frederick Allen, BBC broadcaster, (centre) opened the show which attracted 3,500 people. Pride of place for the council was their own vegetable and fruit exhibit which was 'much admired'.

Bowls in Southall Park, c. 1960. The park boasted bowling greens and tennis courts. Southall Bowls Club was founded in 1901 and was initially based at The White Swan, before making The Wolf its headquarters in 1940. Annual bowling matches had been a regular prewar fixture and were resumed in 1957.

Spikes Bridge sports ground entrance, c. 1930s. It was also known as Southall Municipal Sports Ground and was opened on Saturday 24 July 1937 by Lord Farringdon. The twenty-acre site, which included bowls, cricket and tennis courts, cost the council £21,000. The press referred to the grounds as 'a real oasis for mind and body in an industrial area'.

Cranleigh Gardens in the 1950s. The council purchased 1.91 acres of land for this park in September 1944 at a cost of £903.

Cranleigh Gardens playground, 1950s. A father swings his children in the play area of the park which opened in June 1953. Mr M. Charteris, the play park attendant, organised games for the children, among other duties. Apparently the most popular of the park's attractions were the American Swings.

Southall Carnival, August 1957. An exhibition of Square Dancing on one of the floats. The Foot and Fiddle Club 'brought a very Western touch to the parade. The procession assembled at Adelaide Road and went to the park, via the Broadway and the High Street. The 1957 carnival was part of the Borough's twenty-first anniversary celebrations.

Southall Carnival, August 1959. The mayor, Mr T.J. Steele, talks to the new Carnival Queen, the eighteen-year-old Miss June White, daughter of the licensee of The Three Tuns Public House, whilst she holds her trophy cup. The other girl is Patricia Dalwood, the previous year's Carnival Queen. The mayor remarked, 'Many of our girls are quite modest about their charms … They needn't be.' In the background is Southall Park.

Riders at Norwood Green, November 1962. Although Southall itself was heavily built up with industry and housing, at least since the 1930s, Norwood, up to a point, has preserved its rural charm as a hamlet in Middlesex and this photograph exemplifies it. The house in the background is possibly The Cedars, Tentelow Lane.

Every Milestone near Southall brings us closer.

Two slightly risqué postcards from the Edwardian era. No comment is necessary, except, perhaps, to note the rural ambience. Southall was, in fact, becoming increasingly urbanised at the time.

They say, at Southall, a Miss is as good
as a Mile. I think TWO'S better.